The Greatest Story NEVER Told

The Babe and Jackie

By RAY NEGRON
Illustrated by LAURA SEELEY

Foreword by Clarence B. Jones

HarperCollinsPublishers

To George M. Steinbrenner III and the Steinbrenner Family—
Whose loyalty to the less fortunate of the world
has allowed me to do what I do.
Boss, you made me somebody.
Thank you

To Martin Luther King, Jr., and Father Tom Hartman—
I will continue to share your dreams

To My Staff—
My chief of staff, Theresa Bunger; my man of many hats,
Aris Sakellaridis; and my literary coach, Deni LaMarr.
Without you it just doesn't work

To My Children, Jon-Erik, Joey, Toni, and Ricky—
You have made the biggest sacrifice of all
in order for me to fulfill my dreams.
I love you

The Greatest Story Never Told

Text copyright © 2008 by Ray Negron Illustrations copyright © 2008 by Laura Seeley Printed in the United States of America. All rights reserved. No part of this book may be used or reproduced in any manner whatsoever without written permission except in the case of brief quotations embodied in critical articles and reviews. For information address HarperCollins Children's Books, a division of HarperCollins Publishers, 1350 Avenue of the Americas, New York, NY 10019. www.harpercollinschildrens.com Library of Congress Cataloging-in-Publication Data Negron, Ray. The greatest story never told : the Babe and Jackie / by Ray Negron ; illustrations by Laura Seeley. — 1st ed.   p.   cm.   Summary: Two young boys who are sick in the hospital decide they do not want to be roommates because of their differences, but when they travel back in time and meet Babe Ruth and Jackie Robinson, they change their minds.   ISBN 978-0-06-147161-2 [1. Race relations—Fiction. 2. Friendship—Fiction. 3. Toleration—Fiction. 4. Baseball—Fiction. 5. Ruth, Babe, 1895–1948—Fiction. 6. Robinson, Jackie, 1919–1972—Fiction. 7. Time travel—Fiction.] I. Seeley, Laura L., date, ill. II. Title. PZ7.N421Gr 2008   2007033824   [E]—dc22 CIP AC Typography by Stephanie Bart-Horvath
1 2 3 4 5 6 7 8 9 10 ❖ First Edition

FOREWORD

Nobody told me that the road would be easy,
I don't believe He brought me this far to leave me.
—"I Don't Feel No Ways Tired" by Rev. James Cleveland

The two young boys at the center of *The Greatest Story Never Told* are shown dealing with serious illnesses. Skippy has cancer and Connor has diabetes. These are conditions that can often limit one's physical stamina and abilities. But as you will see, the boys' interest in baseball and in the accomplishments of Babe Ruth and my friend Jackie Robinson are a source of great inspiration to them. That's not surprising, because baseball, like other competitive sports, requires athletes to be the best that they can be. Being afflicted with diabetes, cancer, or any debilitating disease also requires the best of people.

I did not know Babe Ruth, but his love of kids is legendary and his spirit will live forever. I did know Jackie Robinson. I believe there are valuable lessons to be learned from Jackie's career, especially when he became the first black man to play Major League Baseball in 1947.

Jackie Robinson, like the Babe, was a true American hero. He endured with great courage and forbearance all sorts of racial insults and taunts from both fellow players and fans when he first played in the major leagues. Each and every day he walked out onto the baseball field, Jackie committed himself to the pursuit of excellence and played the best that he could in the face of verbal and threatened physical abuse.

And even after he no longer played baseball and became afflicted with diabetes, Jackie Robinson still displayed that quiet, non-complaining self-confidence that exemplified his years as a baseball player. I commend him as a role model for everyone.

—Clarence B. Jones
November 2007

Clarence B. Jones has had a long and distinguished career as a business leader and civil rights activist. During the 1960s, he served as legal counsel and draft speechwriter to the Reverend Martin Luther King, Jr. Mr. Jones is currently a scholar in residence at the Martin Luther King, Jr., Research and Education Institute in Stanford, California, and the author of *What Would Martin Say?*

urse Linda was sitting at the nursing station in the pediatrics unit at Memorial Hospital when she heard a loud commotion coming from room 714. Two of her favorite patients, Skippy and Connor, were fighting. "Well? Which one of you wants to tell me what's going on in here?" she asked.

Skippy answered first. "I want a new roommate!"

"I want a new roommate, too!" Connor replied.

"Oh?" Nurse Linda asked. "And why is that? What's wrong with the two of you sharing a room?"

"Because he's . . . different!" said Connor.

"Yeah, because he's different!" Skippy chimed in.

"Different?" asked Nurse Linda. "Well, let's see. You're both boys, so it can't be that. And you're both very noisy, so that definitely can't be it. Why is Skippy different, Connor? Because he has cancer? Why is Connor different, Skippy? Because he has diabetes?"

"He's just different and I want another roommate," Skippy said angrily.

Nurse Linda looked at Connor. "Can you explain any better?"

Connor just bit his lower lip and dropped his head.

Nurse Linda tucked both of the boys back into their beds. "It's time for your naps, and I don't want to hear another word out of either of you for the next hour. Is that clear? No more of this talk about being different. You both need your rest."

After she left, Connor pulled his blankets over his head and turned onto his left side. Skippy pulled his blankets up and turned onto his right side. They didn't even want to look at each other. Soon, both were fast asleep.

When they woke up, there was someone sitting in a chair between the two beds. Nurse Linda stood behind him, smiling.

The stranger was dressed in a pin-stripe baseball uniform. The boys both eyed him curiously. He smiled at them and tipped his hat. "Pleased to meet both of you. I'm Ray, the batboy."

Linda nodded. "These are the boys I was telling you about, Ray. The ones who want new roommates. I was thinking that you could help them. You know, with some of your . . . magic?"

"Magic?" Skippy said.

Connor's eyes lit up.

Nurse Linda got their clothes. "Well, if you hurry and get dressed, I think I might be able to let you go on a little trip with Ray. Of course, you would have to promise me that you'll be very good. And no fighting!"

"I promise!" Connor cried out.

"Me, too!" said Skippy.

The boys dressed quickly and hurried down the hall with Ray and Nurse Linda. When they came to a side door of the hospital, she opened it and let them out. The boys followed Ray, so excited that they suddenly forgot that they weren't the best of friends.

Before long, they came to a baseball stadium. They both looked at each other and smiled. It was familiar to them. They had seen it on television many times, but today it was empty. Ray led them through the halls until they came to a door that looked like a garage.

As Ray reached down to open the door, a man walked by. "Hello, Ray," he said. "I see you're off on another one of your special trips."

Ray grinned. "Yes, Boss. This is Skippy and Connor. They don't want to share a room anymore because they're different, and I think I know a couple of guys who can help them become friends."

The Boss beamed at the batboy. "Ah, sounds like a good plan to me, pal. I think I know just who you mean, too. Please give them my regards." He winked at Ray and continued down the hall.

As the door rolled open, Ray walked inside. "I'm sorry to have to tell you this, but not only are you going to have to share a room, this time you're going to have to share a chair, too. A very special chair. Hop on, boys—we have somebody to see. Just close your eyes and count backward from ten."

"Ten, nine, eight, seven, six," said Skippy.

"Five, four, three, two, one," said Connor.

10, 9, 8, 7,
6, 5, 4, 3,
2, 1...

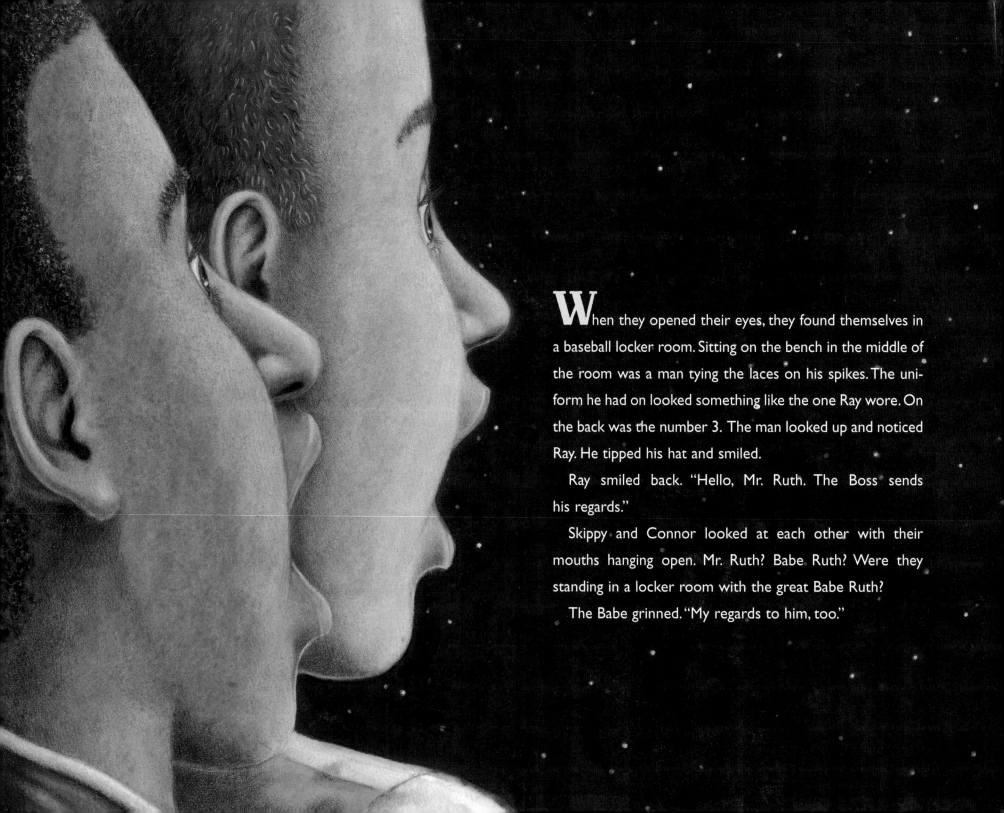

When they opened their eyes, they found themselves in a baseball locker room. Sitting on the bench in the middle of the room was a man tying the laces on his spikes. The uniform he had on looked something like the one Ray wore. On the back was the number 3. The man looked up and noticed Ray. He tipped his hat and smiled.

Ray smiled back. "Hello, Mr. Ruth. The Boss sends his regards."

Skippy and Connor looked at each other with their mouths hanging open. Mr. Ruth? Babe Ruth? Were they standing in a locker room with the great Babe Ruth?

The Babe grinned. "My regards to him, too."

 ust then a man in a black suit with a hat on walked in. He seemed very mad about something.

"There you are, Babe!" he said. "I thought I might find you here. I don't like it, Babe. I don't like it one bit. You can't do this! You can't play against those guys! It just isn't right! It would be bad for baseball. Very bad." He shook his head angrily.

"Well, Mr. Kelly, I'm gonna play anyway," said the Babe.

"Well, they better not beat you or we'll both have a lot of explaining to do." He walked out of the locker room shaking his head. The Babe picked up his glove and motioned for the boys to follow.

he next thing the boys knew, they were sitting in the bleachers watching a baseball game. But it wasn't a big fancy stadium like the ones on television. This was a dusty old field with a baseball diamond in the middle of it and a few rusty bleachers on each side.

"It's 1920 and this is called barnstorming baseball," Ray explained. "The Babe is playing with a bunch of guys from the Majors against a pretty good team from the Negro Leagues." The Babe was batting in the top of the ninth. He hit the ball out of the stadium and the crowd roared as he circled the bases. The score was tied. But the next three batters struck out and the other team came up to bat.

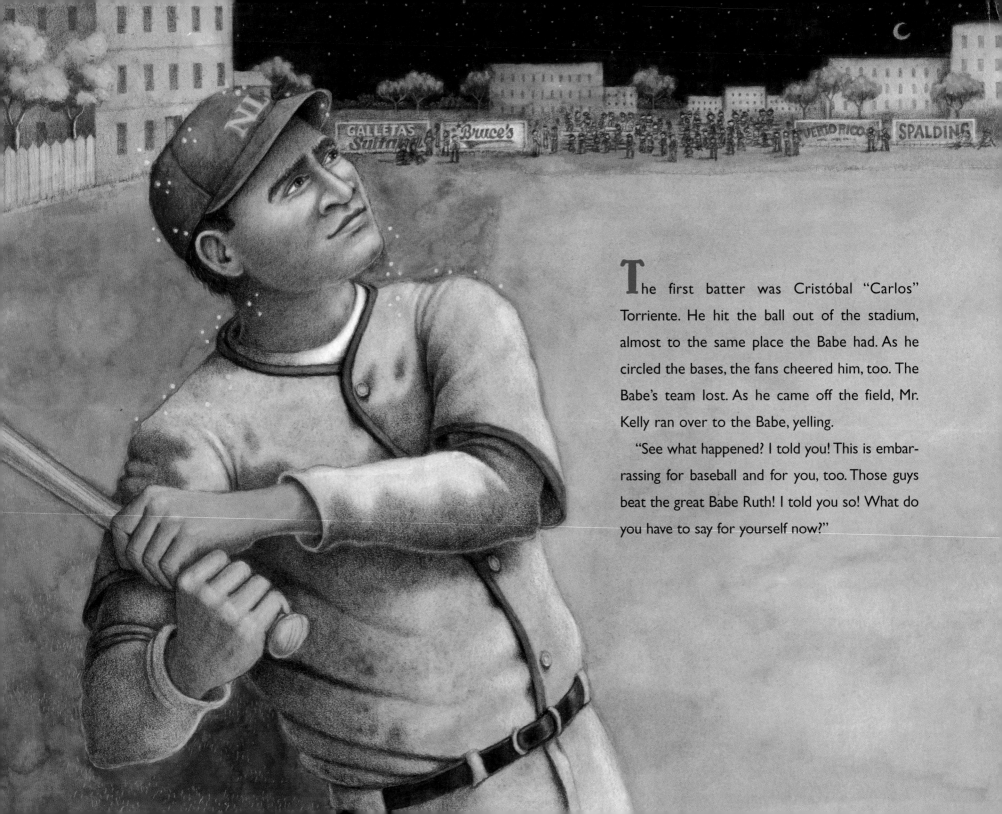

The first batter was Cristóbal "Carlos" Torriente. He hit the ball out of the stadium, almost to the same place the Babe had. As he circled the bases, the fans cheered him, too. The Babe's team lost. As he came off the field, Mr. Kelly ran over to the Babe, yelling.

"See what happened? I told you! This is embarrassing for baseball and for you, too. Those guys beat the great Babe Ruth! I told you so! What do you have to say for yourself now?"

Babe Ruth took off his hat and wiped the sweat off his dusty brow. "I don't know about you, Mr. Kelly, but I'm going to get changed and have a good time celebrating their great game. Carlos promised me some rice and beans, platanos, and some Bustelo coffee. It's a Latino thing—you should try it sometime."

Mr. Kelly shook his head and walked away angrily as Ray tapped the boys on the shoulder. "Come on, guys, we have somewhere else to go."

The next thing the boys knew, they were in another baseball stadium, watching another game. "Today is April 15,
1947," Ray said. "A very special day in baseball history.
Today is the day Jackie Robinson will become the first black
player to play in a Major League game. The Brooklyn
Dodgers are playing the Boston Braves. And over there is
an old friend of ours."

Sitting in the front row was Babe Ruth. In the dugout, the
players were talking and pointing toward the Babe. Slowly,
Jackie Robinson walked up to the top step of the dugout
and tipped his hat in respect. The Babe held up his fist and
mouthed the words "Go get 'em, pal."

Jackie winked at him, gave him a thumbs-up sign, and mouthed back, "Thank you."

Ray tapped the boys on the shoulder again. "Time to go."

"Hey! We just got here!" said Connor.

"Don't we get to stay and see the game?" asked Skippy.

"We have more stops to make. And I promised Nurse Linda I'd have you back in time for dinner." He leaned over and whispered, "Brooklyn wins. Five to three. Jackie scores the winning run."

heir next stop was the hallway of a hospital that looked very much like the one where their room was. "Shh," Ray said. "We have to be very quiet here. It's now 1948 and the Babe is very sick. He's in this room here. Let's look inside."

The Babe opened his eyes and looked at the boys. He smiled at them as they ran to his bed, one on each side. "Hey! What are you guys doing here? Checking up on the Babe?"

"I brought them to see you, Babe," Ray said. "Skippy and Connor are sick, too. They share a room in the hospital, only they can't get along because they're . . . different."

The Babe chuckled and shook his head as he coughed. "The world has no time for those kinds of feelings, Ray.

"In the hospital, huh? Well, in my day, I visited plenty of boys just like you in the hospital. Hit some home runs for them, too. Now, let's see, what's wrong with you guys? The docs taking good care of you?"

"I have diabetes," said Connor.

"And I have cancer," said Skippy.

"So do I, pal, and it's kind of hard for me to talk, but I think I have one more home run left in me.

"Ray, get me my coat and hat over there. If we hurry, we can still make the game."

Ray helped the Babe into his coat and hat. He was weak and moved slowly, but Ray and the boys helped him. "We're going to have to sneak out of here quietly," whispered the Babe in a husky voice. "But don't worry; it's nothing. I've done it before lots of times. I have a friend I have to check up on now and then—just to see how he's doing."

As they walked down the hall, suddenly Skippy and Connor stopped and stared at a nurse in a starched white uniform and a peaked cap. They looked at each other with their mouths open wide. Ray grabbed the two of them and pulled them into the staircase with the Babe.

"Did you see that?" asked Connor.

"That lady looks just like Nurse Linda!" Skippy said.

Ray and the Babe exchanged knowing smiles.

The four of them left the hospital through a side door that looked a lot like the side door at their own hospital. The Babe fished four subway tokens out of his pocket and they hurried to catch the train.

"Where are we going?" asked Connor.

"Yeah, where are you taking us?" asked Skippy.

"We're going to Brooklyn to see a friend of mine," said the Babe.

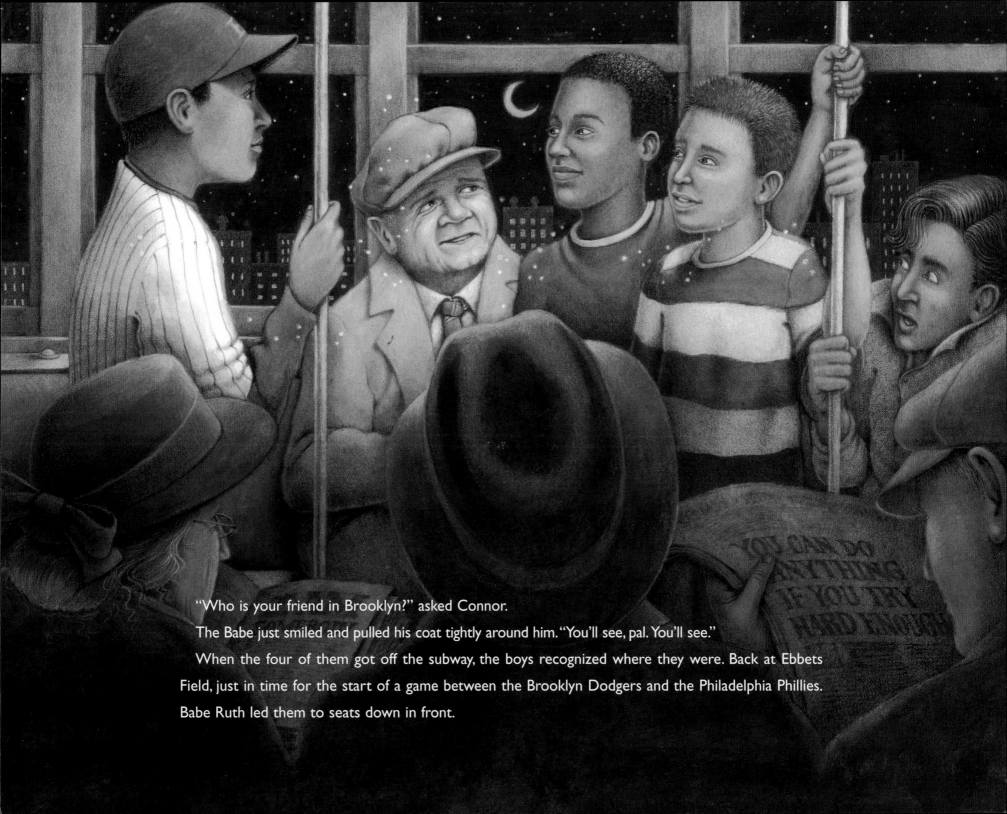

"Who is your friend in Brooklyn?" asked Connor.

The Babe just smiled and pulled his coat tightly around him. "You'll see, pal. You'll see."

When the four of them got off the subway, the boys recognized where they were. Back at Ebbets
Field, just in time for the start of a game between the Brooklyn Dodgers and the Philadelphia Phillies.
Babe Ruth led them to seats down in front.

here's our friend Jackie Robinson," Ray said. "See? He's playing second base."

They watched as the game went on. When the Phillies ran past second base, they were very rough and pushed Jackie around. When they slid into second, they kicked at him and shoved him when they got up. They screamed things at him. But Jackie just played the game and pretended he didn't hear them. The boys looked at the Babe. He shook his head, very sad to see how the other players were treating his friend.

From second base, Jackie noticed the Babe and gave him a wink and a thumbs-up, just like he had the year before. The Babe held up his fist weakly and smiled back.

In the bottom of the ninth inning, Jackie came up to bat. The score was tied. Everyone in the stadium watched anxiously.

The first pitch came in hard and fast and near his head. Jackie fell to the ground as the crowd gasped. He got up slowly, dusting his uniform off, and stepped back up to the plate.

The second pitch was a fastball right over the plate and Jackie swung at it. The ball sailed into the bleachers as the crowd cheered. Jackie and the Dodgers won the game.

s the players walked happily through the tunnel to the locker room, the Babe and the boys waited for Jackie. No one noticed the Babe except for Jackie, who ran right over to him and threw his arms around him. "You're supposed to be very sick, Babe. What are you doing here?"

"Jackie, I brought my friends Skippy and Connor to see you today. They're very sick, too. Only they don't want to share the same room at the hospital because they're, you know, different."

Jackie nodded and smiled at them. "Oh, I see." He put a hand on each of their shoulders. "Let me tell you something, boys. I've learned a lot playing baseball. And one thing I've learned is that you have to count on your teammates—whether they're different or not. It doesn't matter what color their skin is or what color their eyes are—just as long as they're behind you, ready to back you up."

ow did you get here, Babe?" Jackie asked.

Reaching into his coat pocket, the Babe took out a subway token and held it up for Jackie to see. "Same way everyone else gets to Ebbets Field!"

"Well, the great Babe Ruth shouldn't be riding the subway," Jackie said. "Besides, you're sick. I've got a car. I'll drive you back to the hospital just as soon as I change."

Jackie drove back to Memorial Hospital. The Babe sat in the front seat and Ray sat in the back with the boys. The Babe was coughing and very weak. Jackie got out of the car and looked around for help. He spotted a Latino teenage boy walking nearby.

"Hey!" he called out. "Would you mind helping me get my friend back into the hospital?"

The boy's face lit up. "Sure thing, Mr. Robinson. I've seen you play over at Ebbets Field. Sat in the bleachers. You hit a home run that day, too. You're the greatest!"

Jackie smiled. "What's your name, son?"

"Roberto," said the boy as he helped Jackie get the Babe out of the car.

Jackie patted the Babe on the back. "No, Roberto, this is the greatest. This is Babe Ruth."

"Thank you, Mr. Robinson," said Ray. "And by the way, the Boss sends his regards."

Jackie tipped his hat. "Tell him Roberto and I send our regards, too—something tells me we're going to hear about this kid one day."

As the Babe was about to disappear into the hospital with Jackie and Roberto, Connor and Skippy yelled, "We love you, Babe"—at this moment the Babe could only wink. Ray smiled, tapped Skippy and Connor on the shoulder, and said, "Come on, it's time I got you back to your hospital, too."

Later that evening, Nurse Linda heard a loud commotion coming from room 714. Skippy and Connor were yelling again. Only this time, they were sitting on one of the beds side by side, loudly cheering and watching a baseball game on television.

"Well, what is going on in here?" Nurse Linda asked. "I thought the two of you wanted new roommates."

"No way!" Connor said. "I was mean to Skippy, but I'm sorry."

"No, I was mean to Connor," Skippy said, "but now we're friends and teammates."

"Oh? And what brought this change about?" she said.

"We went to this place called Ebbets Field. And we met Babe Ruth," Skippy said.

"And Jackie Robinson was there, too," Connor added. "And there was a lady in a white dress who looked just like you!"

"Wow! That must have been some nap the two of you took!" said Nurse Linda.

As she stepped into the room to turn the television down, the boys spotted Ray walking down the hall with the man he called the Boss and Yankee pitcher Chien-Ming Wang.

"Hi, Nurse Linda! Hi, pals!" said the Boss. "How's everything going in here?" He glanced at the television. "Who's winning?"

Nurse Linda smiled. "Connor and Skippy are."

With the famous Steinbrenner smile, the Boss yelled out, "Atta baby!"

A Note from the Author

Dear Readers,

This book is very dear to my heart because it addresses a subject that has touched my life personally many times—prejudice. As a young boy, when I was told by someone that I didn't belong, I felt like my life was over. The pain was like nothing I had ever experienced. But I was blessed to have some very special people on my side—people like the late Billy Martin, Reggie Jackson, and, most of all, the Boss, George Steinbrenner.

I can remember the Boss telling me not to allow myself to think "that way" and to listen to the words of those who tried to block my path. "If I ever see you bring yourself down to the level of those ignorant people again, you're going to have to deal with my wrath," he told me. And I knew he meant every word of it. Those words meant more to me than I can ever say. They encouraged me to push on and find a place for myself where I could make a difference in this world.

The purpose of this book is to show that you can make a difference by following the examples of Babe Ruth and Jackie Robinson in understanding and accepting all people and treating others with dignity. We need to teach our children those qualities and to learn from the Babe and Jackie never to take their eyes off their dreams and goals.

If I have achieved any amount of success in the world, I know that I owe it mostly to the efforts of George Steinbrenner, who never gave up on me. I know that I am not the only one whom the Boss has reached out to. Being his friend and adviser, I see him do it every day, and this is his true contribution to the world. In my heart and soul, I know that he is a man whose understanding and acceptance for all the children of the world far exceeds what people will ever realize. And that's just the way he wants it.

This is a book to read and discuss with children. Use it to teach them that there are no differences among people that really matter. The physical differences don't mean a thing compared to the person's heart inside.

—Ray Negron
November 2007

A Psychological Overview

How much of our lives is stolen away by misunderstanding, miscommunication, bias, and prejudice? How much of these limited human experiences are caused by worry and doubt, along with an unwillingness to let go? How much do we fail to see what is really there between and among people—especially people from different cultures and ethnicities?

However, how basic and effective it is to observe, listen, and learn from one another. When we allow ourselves to take this positive personal path, our differences become leverage points for cooperation with one another—in school, sports, business, and life.

This story is another outstanding piece of children's literature by Ray Negron. Its points are relevant to children, parents, athletes, and business executives. It highlights the importance of being in the moment, interacting with one another, and supporting each other. The story hits a home run with its points about appreciating differences, encouraging teamwork, and engaging in life the right way.

The author uses the sport of baseball and links the game to the life experiences of two young chronically ill boys. In using Hall of Fame players Babe Ruth and Jackie Robinson as characters and mentors to these boys, Ray Negron makes important points about how people from diverse races, dispositions, and time periods can get along and assist one another—if they just believe and let it happen.

This book will stand the test of time. It offers creative and real ways of promoting quality multicultural living, on and off the baseball diamond. It needs a roster spot in the home, clubhouse, school, and office. It can be called upon for guidance and inspiration on a regular basis.

—Dr. Charlie Maher
Team Psychologist, Cleveland Indians
and Professor of Psychology
Graduate School of Applied and Professional Psychology
Rutgers University

Acknowledgments

This book would not be possible without the help and inspiration of the following people and organizations:

Tom Hopke, Laura Seeley, Melanie Donovan, Theresa Bunger, Angela Valdez, Michael Valdez, Cirilo & Ventura Negron, Nancy Negron, Amanda Hill, Michael Windishman Jr., Naomi & Michael Windishman, Malcolm Valdez, Barbara & Jerry Delorenzo, Lt. Kelli Webb, Brenda Bonini, Adele Smithers, Father Tom Hartman, Connor Dromerhauser, the Dromerhauser Family, Mort Fleishner, Aris Sakellaridis, Josh Zeide, Debbie Medina, Alfred Zaccagnino, Deni LaMarr, the New York Yankees, the Steinbrenner Family, Felix Lopez, Randy & Mindy Levine, Manny Garcia, Brian Cashman, Raquel Julich, Cesar Presbott, Robert Brown, Omar Minaya, Willie & Gretchen Randolph, Ron Dock, Bobby & Kay Murcer, Todd Murcer, Vincent Kenyon, Hector Pagan, Jim Madorma, Joseph Kenyon, Joey Gian, Tom Giordano, Roberto Alomar & family, Reggie Jackson ("Mr. October"), Mr. & Mrs. Ray Aguila, Puerto Rico USA Imports, Sy Presten, Lenny Caro, the Bronx Chamber of Commerce, Bruce Zipes, Bruce's Bakery, David Jurist, Hackensack University Medical Center, Geri Barish, Ellen Hirschbein, Hewlett House, the Giovinazzo Family, James Lanzarotta, Andy & Linda Ruth Tosetti, the Bunger Family, Chris Rohrbaugh, the Lou Gehrig Family, Julio Pabon, Byron Hunter, Latino Sports, Carl Ferraro, Robert Narvaez, Spalding, Regent Sports, Darryl & Tracy Strawberry, Phil Tavella & family, Mike Capobianco & family, the Hess Family, the LaValva Family, Larry Holmes, the Bunger Surf Shop, Dave Valle, Charlie Maher, Jack Szigety, Stephen Walker, Bob Klapisch, Jon Heyman, Scott Clark, Steve Serbe, Ken Davidoff, Dan Graziano, George King, Kevin Kiernan, Russ Salzberg, Jack Curry, Juan Gonzalez, John Harper, Michael Max Knobbe, Bronx Net, Robinson Cano, Ron Villone, Chien-Ming Wang, Café Bustelo, Eddie Torres, Galletas Sultana, Danny Masiello, Ameriprise, Phil Pursino, Joe DeSena, Daniel Quintero, the Kips Bay Boys & Girls Club, James Fiorentino, Fritz Coudert, Tom Muir, Luis Antonio Ramos, April Lee Hernandez, Alexander Garret, Luis Guzmán, Jim Leyritz, Michael Kay, Marvell Scott, Bill Ritter, Xiomara Medina, Casper Martinez, Rich Ramirez, Don Cooper, Steve Kalafer, Tom & Debbie Delfranco, Vaughn D. Dean, Barbara Connolly, Stephen Kyrkostas, Ken Fagan, Christine Mathews, Anthony Epps, the Unger Family, Ben Morelli, Frankie Valli, Deirdre & Don Imus, George N. Tim, Miguel Montas, La Caridad, Richard Seko, Chris Ruddy, Fred Cambria, Terri Jenkins, Mary Pollino, the Babe Ruth Family, the Creative Group, Joe Avallone, Mike Kostel, Adolfo Carrion Jr., the Roger Maris Family, Judith Wells, Kathy Bennett, Tony Morante, Josephine Doring, Donna Valenti, Bobby Rossi, Billy Martin Jr., Juan Vene, the Gooden Family, Steve Fortunato, Shirley Beauchamp, Memorial Sloan-Kettering, Columbia Presbyterian, Andy Garcia, Lou Iacucci, Jim MacGilvray, Chris Lewis, Rose Rodriguez, P.S. 55, Luis Torres, UPS, Tug McGraw, Billy Berroa, Beto Villa, the N.Y. Latin Press Corps, Howard Grosswirth, John Szponar, Stacie & Tony Rodriguez, Bethpage Federal Credit Union, Joann Nastell, the Chuck Feinstein Family, Kenwal Day Camp, Lord & Taylor, José Feliciano, Promesa, Felix Millan, the Roberto Clemente Family, Mead Chasky, Harold Reynolds, Reed Bergman, Jackie William, Diane Blanco, the Mickey Mantle Family, Paul McCartney, Richard & Homer Gere, Frank Sinatra, Sammy Davis Jr., Martin Luther King, Jr., and Elston Howard, the first black Yankee (1955).